A LIVING LEGACY:
HISTORIC STRINGED INSTRUMENTS
AT
THE JUILLIARD SCHOOL

A Living Legacy:
Historic Stringed Instruments
at
The Juilliard School

Author and Editor
Lisa B. Robinson

Foreword
Itzhak Perlman

AMADEUS
PRESS

787
L785

The Juilliard School gratefully acknowledges the underwriters of this publication,
Mr. and Mrs. Lester S. Morse, Jr.

Published in 2006 by The Juilliard School

Published by arrangement with
Amadeus Press, LLC
512 Newark Pompton Turnpike
Pompton Plains, NJ 07444

For sales, please contact

NORTH AMERICA

AMADEUS PRESS, LLC
c/o Hal Leonard Corp.
7777 West Bluemound Road
Milwaukee, WI 53213, USA
Tel. 800-637-2852
Fax 414-774-3259
E-mail: orders@amadeuspress.com
Website: www.amadeuspress.com

UNITED KINGDOM AND EUROPE

ROUNDHOUSE PUBLISHING LTD.
Millstone, Limers Lane
Northam, North Devon EX39 2RG, UK
Phone: 01237-474474
Fax: 01237-474774
E-mail: roundhouse.group@ukgateway.net

Cover Design and Interior Design: Donald Giordano
Photographs reproduced with permission of Tucker Densley

Printed in the United States of America

Library of Congress Cataloging-in-Publication Data

Living legacy : historic stringed instruments at the Juilliard School /
edited by Lisa B. Robinson ; Foreword by Itzhak Perlman.
    p. cm.
  Includes bibliographical references and index.
  ISBN 1-57467-146-4 (alk. paper)
  1. Bowed stringed instruments--Catalogs and collections--New York
(State)--New York. 2. Juilliard School--Musical instrument collections. I. Robinson,
Lisa Brooks.

  ML462.N5J85 2006
  787'.190747471--dc22

2006009410

TABLE OF CONTENTS

ACKNOWLEDGMENTS

ONE OF THE myriad pleasures of assembling this book was the chance to work more closely with several Juilliard colleagues and collaborate with a number of other exceptional individuals from outside the school. I am deeply grateful to all those named here for their contributions. I also wish to thank Joseph W. Polisi, President of The Juilliard School, for the opportunity to take on this challenging and rewarding project.

My most profound debt of gratitude goes to Eric Grossman, the curator of Juilliard's stringed instrument collection. Eric was an indispensable source of information and deftly handled the complex logistics of arranging the photography. This book would not exist were it not for the countless hours he spent helping bring it to life. Tucker Densley's stunning photography reveals the featured instruments to a degree of detail I hadn't thought possible, while Donald Giordano's exquisite design serves as a perfect complement to the beauty of the instruments themselves.

I extend my sincere thanks to Robert Bein for generously sharing his research on several of the instruments, to René Morel for his encouragement and expertise, and to Isaac Salchow for his assistance with the bow descriptions. Two colleagues at Juilliard, Michael Maione and Awoye Timpo, kindly assisted with the deciphering and translation of several documents related to the Guadagnini *ex Ysaÿe*. Stephen Clapp, Dean of The Juilliard School, lent his expert advice and unqualified support to the project. Karen Raven, Juilliard's Director of Major and Planned Gifts, offered many pertinent suggestions. I also wish to thank Jane Gottlieb, Juilliard's Vice President for Library and Information Resources, for her warm guidance and assistance in preparing the bibliography, and Jeni Dahmus, Juilliard's archivist, for her professionalism and patience when I repeatedly asked to view materials "just one more time, I promise!"

Finally, on behalf of the entire Juilliard community, I would like to offer a very special thank you to Mr. and Mrs. Lester S. Morse, Jr. for their generous support in underwriting the cost of producing this book.

FOREWORD

T UCKED AWAY AT the end of one of Juilliard's labyrinthine corridors lies a vault that houses a hidden treasure: the School's outstanding collection of rare stringed instruments. At any given time, many of those instruments are checked out to appreciative students through Juilliard's actively utilized Instrumental Loan Program, which allows the School's artists to borrow appropriate instruments for major performances and competitions. Unlike those in museums, which are mainly displayed as artifacts, Juilliard's collection is truly a "living legacy," as the title of this book indicates. Indeed, the true measure of the collection's value is not its substantial monetary worth, but its availability as a resource for the many talented young string players at Juilliard who lack a performance-quality instrument. I should know, since I was one such student when I won the Levintritt Competition in 1964 with the 1731 Guarneri del Gesù on loan from the collection! Today, as a teacher in Juilliard's Pre-College and College Divisions, I'm grateful that my own students have the opportunity to borrow instruments through this invaluable program.

This handsome book formally documents the collection, which currently includes more than 200 instruments, and showcases 25 of its most important instruments – along with several bows – through vivid descriptions and photographs of stunning clarity. Certificates of authenticity and other documents for several of the collection's most distinguished violins are featured in the appendix, while Ms. Robinson's introductory material provides relevant overviews of the Instrumental Loan Program and the history of Juilliard and its String Department.

The legendary violinist Fritz Kreisler once said, "A good instrument may be defined as one that puts the least impediment in the way of expression. Bad instruments are obstructive, like shaky bridges or physical barriers that stand between you and your destination." Juilliard is indeed fortunate to have such an exceptional collection of stringed instruments for its students to utilize during this formative stage of their artistic journeys, and it is a pleasure to share them with you through this volume.

Itzhak Perlman
Dorothy Richard Starling Foundation Chair in Violin
The Juilliard School

A BRIEF HISTORY OF
THE JUILLIARD SCHOOL

T*HROUGHOUT ITS HISTORY,* The Juilliard School has maintained a commitment to providing the highest caliber of artistic and educational training to exceptionally talented young performing artists from around the world. Juilliard was founded in 1905 as the Institute of Musical Art by Dr. Frank Damrosch, the godson of Franz Liszt and the head of music education for New York City's public schools. Damrosch felt that the most gifted American musicians should not have to go abroad for advanced study, and envisioned the Institute as an American music academy that would provide training comparable to that of the established European conservatories. With enrollment figures rapidly climbing to nearly five times what was expected, the Institute quickly outgrew its original home at Fifth Avenue and moved to new quarters near Columbia University in 1910.

Nine years later, a wealthy textile merchant named Augustus Juilliard died and left in his will the largest single bequest for the advancement of music at that time. The trustees of the bequest founded the Juilliard Graduate School in 1924 to help worthy music students complete their education. In 1926, the Graduate School and the Institute of Musical Art merged, and two years later the distinguished Columbia University professor John Erskine became President of the combined institutions. Erskine was succeeded in 1937 by renowned concert pianist and composer Ernest Hutcheson, who served in the position until 1945.

Succeeding Hutcheson in 1945, composer William Schuman expanded Juilliard's identity as a conservatory devoted exclusively to musical training with the establishment of the Dance Division, under the direction of Martha Hill, in 1951. In 1968, during the tenure of Peter Mennin (appointed President in 1962), a Drama Division was created, with John Houseman as its first director and Michel Saint-Denis as consultant. The School changed its name to The Juilliard School to reflect its broader artistic scope, and moved to its current home at Lincoln Center the following year. The first production of The Juilliard Opera Center, Igor Stravinsky's *The Rake's Progress,* celebrated the opening of the Juilliard Theater (now the Peter Jay Sharp Theater) at Lincoln Center in 1970.

Following Mennin's death in 1983, Dr. Joseph W. Polisi became the School's sixth and current President, beginning with the 1984-85 academic year. During his administration, Juilliard realized a major goal in the completion of the Meredith Willson Residence Hall, which opened in 1990. The opening of the residence hall, along with a strengthened liberal arts program and an increasing emphasis on community service, reflect the current administration's desire to respond to the needs of its students and the community at large while maintaining the highest standards in performing arts education. In September 2001, Juilliard inaugurated a comprehensive jazz studies program developed in partnership with Jazz at Lincoln Center.

The most compelling measure of Juilliard's success can be seen in the achievements of its alumni, whose many familiar names include musicians Van Cliburn, Yo-Yo Ma, Itzhak Perlman, and Leontyne Price; dancers Martha Clarke, Pina Bausch, and Paul Taylor; and actors Christine Baranski, Kevin Kline, Patti LuPone, and Robin Williams. More than twenty percent of the personnel of the six leading American orchestras are Juilliard graduates, as are members of many of the world's leading chamber music ensembles.

JUILLIARD'S STRING DEPARTMENT

FROM ITS EARLIEST years, The Juilliard School has maintained a distinguished roster of noted pedagogues. The Institute of Musical Art faculty included violinist Franz Kneisel and other members of the Kneisel Quartet, the first professional string quartet in the United States. Among Kneisel's students was Joseph Fuchs, who joined the faculty in 1946 and served as one of the School's most esteemed and best-loved teachers until the time of his death in 1997 at the age of 97. Other eminent violin teachers during Juilliard's early decades included Edouard Dethier, Leopold Auer, and Louis Persinger. Dethier joined the faculty in 1906 and served for an astonishing 56 years, teaching talented students such as Robert Mann, one of the founding members of the Juilliard String Quartet and a distinguished member of Juilliard's current faculty. Leopold Auer, whose students included Jascha Heifetz and Mischa Elman, was appointed in 1918 and served until his death in 1930, when he was replaced by Louis Persinger, another noted pedagogue whose many gifted students during his 36-year tenure included international concert soloists Isaac Stern and Ruggiero Ricci.

Further solidifying Juilliard's reputation for excellence in the training of talented young string players, in 1946 the legendary violin pedagogue Ivan Galamian was appointed to the faculty. As one of the most influential violin teachers of the 20th century, Galamian trained hundreds of students during his 35 years on the faculty, many of whom went on to important careers as soloists, chamber and orchestral musicians, and teachers – several of them at Juilliard. Those students included such prominent violinists as Pinchas Zukerman, Kyung-Wha Chung, Jaime Laredo, Miriam Fried, and Glenn Dicterow, concertmaster of the New York Philharmonic. Another of those students was Dorothy DeLay, who served as Galamian's chief assistant for the 20 years from 1946-1966 and became one of the world's most respected and beloved violin teachers, fostering the unique talents of outstanding violinists such as Itzhak Perlman, Nadja Salerno-Sonnenberg, Schlomo Mintz, Cho-Liang Lin, Midori, and Nigel Kennedy. Miss DeLay held the Dorothy Richard Starling Foundation Chair in Violin from the time of its establishment in 1997 until her death in 2002. Mr. Perlman, who joined the faculty in 1999, was appointed to the position in 2003.

Another influential teacher in Juilliard's String Department was cellist Leonard Rose. Serving on the faculty from 1947 to 1984, Mr. Rose taught Yo-Yo Ma, Lynn Harrell, and current Juilliard faculty member Fred Sherry, among other notable artists. Among Juilliard's viola faculty, two historically significant teachers were Paul Doktor, who taught at Juilliard from 1971 until his death in 1989, and Karen Tuttle, who joined the faculty in 1987 and retired in 2003. Juilliard's string faculty also included two of America's leading double bass teachers: David Walter, who taught at the School from 1969 until his retirement in 2002, and Homer Mensch, who joined the faculty in 1970 and taught until his death in 2005.

Juilliard is proud to have been home to the Juilliard String Quartet, recognized as one of the world's leading chamber ensembles, since the time of its founding in 1946. Current members of the Quartet are Joel Smirnoff, who joined the group as second violinist in 1986 and replaced Robert Mann as first violinist when Mann retired in 1997; Ronald Copes, who joined as second violinist in 1997; Samuel Rhodes, the Quartet's violist since 1969; and cellist Joel Krosnick, who replaced his former teacher, Claus Adam, in 1974. In addition to teaching private students individually, the Quartet provides intensive coaching and career preparation for promising young string quartets that are accepted as pre-formed ensembles into a special Artist Diploma program. Some of the notable groups that have participated in the program include the Tokyo, Emerson, American, LaSalle, Miró, and St. Lawrence quartets.

With 37 faculty members and close to 250 students, or about one-third of the total student enrollment, Juilliard's String Department is now the School's largest. Students come from all over the world to study with members of a faculty that includes internationally acclaimed soloists, world-renowned chamber and orchestral musicians, and leading pedagogues. Juilliard's String Department offers the Bachelor of Music, Master of Music, and Doctor of Musical Arts degrees, as well as the Artist Diploma in Performance or String Quartet Studies.

OVERVIEW OF JUILLIARD'S
STRINGED INSTRUMENT COLLECTION

T*HE JUILLIARD SCHOOL'S* Stringed Instrument Collection exists primarily as a result of the exceptional generosity of individuals who, over the years, have wished to benefit the School and see their instruments put to active use. Thanks to these donors and others whose generous bequests have allowed Juilliard to purchase additional instruments, the School now has a collection of stringed instruments – mainly violins, but also violas, cellos, and double basses – numbering more than 200, as well as numerous bows. The collection includes several instruments by the two great Cremonese masters Antonio Stradivari and Giuseppi Guarneri del Gesù, as well as fine examples by Amati, Bergonzi, Gagliano, Guadagnini, and others.

This catalogue presents an annotated list of important instruments in the collection, with photographs and descriptions of 25 instruments and three bows of special historical interest. These include a Stradivarius violin that once belonged to a Russian czar and was later owned by Avery Fisher; a Guarneri del Gesù violin played by a member of the Viennese quartet that premiered many of Beethoven's and Schubert's works in that genre; and a Stradivarius cello previously owned by Hugo Becker, head of the Berlin Hochschule für Musik. Copies of relevant certificates of authenticity for several of the most important instruments are reproduced in the Appendix. A bibliography of materials on historical instruments, prepared with the assistance of Jane Gottlieb, Juilliard's Vice President for Library and Information Resources, is also included.

ERIC GROSSMAN

Violinist Eric Grossman has been Curator of The Juilliard School's Stringed Instrument Collection since 1986.

Mr. Grossman's first teacher was his father, cellist John Grossman, who instilled in him an abiding love for music. A graduate of Juilliard, where he studied with Dorothy DeLay and Masao Kawasaki, Mr. Grossman enjoys an active performing career. He has given highly acclaimed recitals and solo performances with orchestras in the U.S., Europe, Korea, Japan, and Cuba under renowned conductors including Zubin Mehta, Stanislaw Skrowaczewski, and Michael Gielen. In 2004, Mr. Grossman gave the New York premiere of Lowell Liebermann's Concerto for Violin, Piano and String Quartet and has also performed and recorded Liebermann's Violin Sonata with the composer. In 2006, he is scheduled to play the world premiere of a concerto written for him by composer Jorge Lopéz Marin with the Orquesta Sinfonica Nacional de Cuba in Havana.

As a chamber musician, Mr. Grossman has collaborated with such noted artists as David Soyer, Seymour Lipkin, Philip Myers, and Sandra Rivers, among many others; and as an Artistic Director of the Cosmopolitan Chamber Players, he oversees an annual concert series at Merkin Concert Hall in New York. In 2005-06, Mr. Grossman will present the complete unaccompanied sonatas and partitas of Bach and Ysaÿe's six sonatas as part of a teaching and performance residency at Minnesota State University in Moorhead.

The Instrumental Loan Program

The main purpose of the Stringed Instrument Collection is to provide instruments for student use through the Instrumental Loan Program. This important program allows students in Juilliard's College and Pre-College divisions to borrow instruments to use for occasions, such as public performances or competitions, for which their own instruments are inadequate. It also serves the vital function of providing longer term loans for students in need of a better quality practice instrument. Given the high cost of performance-quality stringed instruments, especially violins, the Instrumental Loan Program meets a crucial need among students in Juilliard's String Division, who make up approximately one-third of the School's total enrollment. Over the years, hundreds of students – including well-known artists such as Itzhak Perlman, Sarah Chang and Gil Shaham (alumni of Juilliard's Pre-College Division), Angella Ahn, Catherine Cho, and Anna Rabinova, who used the School's 1775 Guadagnini for her successful audition for the New York Philharmonic – have benefited from the program.

Juilliard takes every precaution to ensure the safety of the instruments in the collection. Students who wish to borrow an instrument are required to sign a loan agreement stipulating that they will abide by the specific conditions of the agreement and be wholly responsible for the safety and care of the instrument for the duration of the loan. When not signed out to students, instruments are housed in a climate-constant vault with specially designed shelving, and their condition is regularly monitored by the curator, Eric Grossman. Repairs are made by René A. Morel, whose innovative restoration methods and meticulous craftsmanship have made him one of the world's most respected and influential luthiers. His shop, Morel & Gradoux-Matt Inc., is located near Juilliard on New York City's Upper West Side.

Donating an Instrument to Juilliard

Juilliard enthusiastically welcomes donations of quality stringed instruments, which are in constant demand by students in both the College and Pre-College divisions. Very few of the talented young artists who attend Juilliard have instruments that complement their musicality and technical mastery, and having the opportunity to practice and perform on a better instrument can have a truly transformational effect on their playing. Donors can be assured that their gift will provide tremendous benefit to Juilliard and its students for years to come.

Individuals interested in donating an instrument to the School are encouraged to contact the Office of the Dean, at (212) 799-5000 ext. 204, or the Office of Development and Public Affairs, at (212) 799-5000 ext. 278. Donors who wish to remain anonymous may do so with Juilliard's full assurance of confidentiality.

INSTRUMENTS OF
SPECIAL HISTORICAL SIGNIFICANCE

I.

ANTONIO STRADIVARI

(1692)

AVERY FISHER

M ADE DURING STRADIVARI'S so-called "long period" of 1690-1698, during which he experimented with larger dimensions that may have been influenced by the works of Giovanni Paolo Maggini[1], the *Avery Fisher* violin is nonetheless a conventional size of 14 inches in length. A description of the instrument in a 1976 issue of *The Strad* cites its "Amati-like elegance" and "graceful outline, exquisitely cut f-holes and delicately wrought details." The varnish is a deep golden-brown color.

The earliest known history of this instrument maintains that it was given by the Czar of Russia to his court violinist, Eugene Maria Albrecht (1842-1894). After Albrecht's death, the instrument was sold by his widow and brought to England. In 1905 it was sold by William E. Hill & Sons to Lady (Dorothy) Fleetwood-Hesketh, an accomplished amateur musician. After her death the instrument was passed on to her daughter, Miss Joan Fleetwood-Hesketh. The violin remained in Miss Fleetwood-Hesketh's possession until her death in 1975, when it was put up for sale by order of her executors and purchased by Avery Fisher from Christie's in 1976. Mr. Fisher donated the violin to Juilliard on the occasion of his 85th birthday in 1991. His announcement of the gift concluded with the magnanimous wish that the violin would "bring joy and inspiration to endless generations of talented Juilliard students and their audiences."

---

[1] W. Henry, Arthur F., and Alfred E. Hill, *Antonio Stradivari: His Life and Work* (London: William E. Hill & Sons, 1902; reprint, New York: Dover Publications, Inc., 1963), 43.

II.

ANTONIO STRADIVARI

(1728)

ARTÔT

THIS VIOLIN IS named after Belgian violinist Alexandre Artôt (1815-1845), the first owner to whom it can be traced. Subsequent owners included a M. Falcon of Paris and the French luthier Emile Germain. M. Germain had possession of the instrument from 1897 until 1902, when it was purchased by William E. Hill & Sons and sold to a J.A.W. Häck of the Hague. After being sold by Mr. Häck to a Mr. van Cricht of Antwerp in 1914, the violin was next sold in 1938 to acclaimed pianist and composer Leopold Godowsky by Emil Hermann. It was donated to Juilliard by Leopold Godowsky, Jr. in 1959.

Made by Stradivari at the age of 84, the Hill certificate from 1902 (reproduced in the Appendix) describes the violin as characteristic in style and material of those made from 1725-1730, when Stradivari was still "producing specimens of the highest order."[1] The back is made from two pieces of maple, with plainer sides and head; the length is 13 15/16 inches and the varnish a vivid reddish color.

[1] Ibid., 81.

III.

GIUSEPPE GUARNERI DEL GESÙ

(1729)

PIXIS

THIS VIOLIN WAS donated to Juilliard by Howard Phipps, Jr. in 2000. The instrument takes its name from its first known owner, Friedrich Wilhelm Pixis (1785-1842), a violinist, composer, and teacher who studied under noted violin pedagogue and composer Giovanni Battista Viotti. The instrument was purchased by William E. Hill & Sons from a French violinist, Alfred Louis Turban, around 1880 and was sold around 1885 to Mr. Gilbert Watson. In 1892, the instrument was sold through Hill to Fridolin Hamma, a well-known German instrument dealer. That same year, Mr. Hamma sold the violin to a Mr. Kessler of Berlin, who then sold it to noted American violinist Theodore Spiering, concertmaster of the New York Philharmonic under Mahler. The instrument was later acquired by Nathan E. Posner, a collector, and sold to Mr. John Hudson Bennett sometime during the late 1920s or early 1930s. According to Mr. Phipps, Jr., his father (in consultation with his uncle, John S. Phipps, a violin collector) purchased the instrument in 1943 for his musically gifted son from Mr. Bennett's widow, Katherine D. Bennett. (According to an announcement from the American Art Association's Anderson Galleries in New York, Mr. Bennett's entire collection was put up for sale in 1932, but in light of Mr. Phipps's account, the instrument was presumably not purchased.)

As noted in the program for the Anderson Galleries sale, the dimensions of the instrument are as follows: Length, 13 3/4 inches; upper bout width, 6 1/2 inches; lower bout width, 8 1/16 inches; middle bout width, 4 5/16 inches; string length, 12 7/8 inches. The top is made from close-grained wood and the back from one piece of broad curly maple, with sides to match. The varnish is a beautiful red shade. The program also notes that "This violin is an example of the more finished work of its great maker and is notable for the unusual thickness of its back, resulting in an unusually massive tone like that of the great del Gesù used by the late Eugène Ysaÿe."

Before donating the violin to Juilliard, Mr. Phipps, Jr. enjoyed playing the instrument himself for many years, and more recently had loaned it for a period of time to Juilliard alumna Ani Kavafian. As part of Juilliard's Instrumental Loan Program, it has been used by Yi-Jia Susanne Hou and Tai Murray.

IV.

GIUSEPPE GUARNERI DEL GESÙ

CREMONA (1731)

MAYSEDER GUARNERIUS

T*HE SUCCESSION OF* artists who have owned and performed on this violin reveals an illustrious history. The instrument is named after its first known owner, Joseph Mayseder (1789-1863), a member of Vienna's famed Schuppanzigh Quartet. Subsequently owned by American concert violinist Maud Powell (1867-1920), it came to Juilliard in 1952 as an anonymous gift.

A letter of 1903 from Arthur F. Hill to Maud Powell (reproduced in the Appendix) recounts that the instrument had been sold to Mr. Hill's father sometime around 1868-1873 by a clergyman named Waldy, who repurchased it a few years later and sold it to a violinist, Mr. Charles Fletcher. After a few more years it passed to an amateur, Captain Harvey, who then sold it to British violin maker George Hart. Mr. Hart sold it to a Mr. Robert Crawford of Edinburgh, from whom it was purchased by Hill in 1902. In 1903 it was bought from Hill by Ms. Powell, who played it for several years before selling it around 1913 to an A.J. Jones of Springfield, Illinois. An entry in Arthur Hill's diary observes that the violin "always had a fine tone" despite its appearance as a "much worn and somewhat plain looking instrument."[1]

As part of Juilliard's Instrumental Loan Program, this instrument was loaned to Itzhak Perlman when he was a student. As noted in his foreword to this book, this was the violin played by Mr. Perlman when he won first place in the prestigious Levintritt Competition in 1964. The instrument was also used by noted violinist Gil Shaham while he was a student in Juilliard's Pre-College Division.

[1] Arthur F. Hill, *Diaries, 1890-1939* (London: Unpublished), cited in written note to the author from Robert Bein.

V.

GIUSEPPE GUARNERI DEL GESÙ

(1731-34)

EX GENEVA

THIS HISTORIC INSTRUMENT has been generously promised to Juilliard by Louise Behrend through a gift in her will. Ms. Behrend has been a member of Juilliard's Pre-College faculty since 1948 and its College faculty since 1999. She has owned the violin since 1963, when she purchased it from Jacques Français.

In the possession of the Turrettini family of Geneva for more than 150 years, the violin was played during that time by such legendary violinists as Vieuxtemps, Joachim, and Ysaÿe when they visited the city. A note written in 1934 by John R. Dubbs of Lyon & Healy, who had acquired the instrument by that time, further relates that "Some time ago I had a number of our choicest violins at Nashville, and while there I met the distinguished opera conductor, [Alexander] Savine. The minute he saw the Guarnerius he exclaimed, 'Did this not belong to the Turrettini family of Geneva?' I assured him that it had. He then said to me, 'This violin brings back to me a very fond recollection, for many years ago when I was conducting opera at Geneva I had the pleasure of hearing the great Spanish violinist, Pablo de Sarasate, playing his concert upon this instrument.'"

The violin was bought from Lyon & Healy in 1943 by E. Clem Wilson of Los Angeles. A Lyon & Healy certificate prepared for the 1943 sale characterizes the instrument as "one of the most beautiful examples from the hand of this maker that has ever graced our collection." The physical description notes that "The back is of one piece of beautiful maple with sides to match. The top is of spruce of fine grain and of the choicest quality for tone. The scroll is in the master's finest style, and the varnish is of a lovely golden red color." The violin is 13 15/16 inches in length.

VI.

GIUSEPPE GUARNERI DEL GESÙ
(1740-1743)

DUC DE CAMPOSELICE

THIS VIOLIN IS named for its first known owner, a Belgian musician named Victor Reubsaet who was granted the Vatican title "Duke of Camposelice" after his marriage to Isabella Eugenia Singer, the third wife and widow of Isaac Merritt Singer (inventor of the famed sewing-machine model). According to a 1928 certificate of authenticity from Lyon & Healy, the instrument was acquired by the Duke in Florence. It was sold to a Mr. Belouet of Paris by the Duchess (Isabella Eugenia) in 1890 and was purchased by the well-known collector Dwight J. Partello in 1904. In 1928 the instrument was put up for sale by Lyon & Healy, whose certificate characterizes it as "one of the choicest violins from the hand of this master known to us." The individual who purchased it from Lyon & Healy donated the violin to Juilliard anonymously in 1953. Loaned to violinist Sarah Chang during her studies in Juilliard's Pre-College Division, this was the instrument Ms. Chang played for her 1994 debut with the Berlin Philharmonic.

As indicated on the 1904 certificate from William E. Hill & Sons (reproduced in the Appendix), the violin is made in a similar style to the famous "Vieuxtemps" of 1741, an instrument allusive of the Brescian school of violin making. The back of the instrument is made of two pieces of flamed maple, with matching sides and neck, and the top is made from medium grain spruce. The violin measures 13 15/16 inches in length and has a golden varnish.

VII.

PIETRO GUARNERI OF VENICE

(1721)

GRIMSON GUARNERI

THIS VIOLIN, MADE by the brother of Giuseppe Guarneri del Gesù, was donated to Juilliard in 1956 by Mrs. Samuel Grimson (Dr. Bettina Warburg), a prominent psychoanalyst and niece of James Loeb, the principal benefactor of the Institute of Musical Art, Juilliard's predecessor institution. It had been purchased from William E. Hill & Sons in 1949 by Mr. Grimson, a concert violinist and Juilliard alumnus. A letter accompanying the certificate of authenticity provides this colorful history: "It belonged for many years to a Mr. Wolfmanis, a resident of St. Petersburg, prior to the First World War. After suffering imprisonment at the hands of the Bolsheviks, he emigrated to Paris; it was on one of his occasional visits to London, that we first saw the instrument. He ultimately went to South America, where he died, the violin passing into the hands of his son-in-law, Mr. Connus, from whom we acquired the instrument some few years ago."

As noted in the certificate from William E. Hill & Sons (reproduced in the Appendix), this violin is one of the few made by Pietro Guarneri in Cremona. The back is in one piece and the instrument is varnished in a reddish-brown color. Its length is 14 1/16 inches.

VIII.

GIOVANNI GRANCINO

(1699)

THIS VIOLA WAS purchased by Juilliard from Jacques Français in 1956. The certificate of authenticity indicates that the instrument was previously owned by Berlin banker and instrument collector Franz von Mendelssohn, who later gave it to his son-in-law Emil Bohnke (1888-1928), a violinist and composer of chamber music whose life was tragically cut short by an automobile accident. While the certificate asserts that Bohnke was a member of the famous Joachim String Quartet, he in fact served from 1919-21 as the violist of the Busch String Quartet, an ensemble also renowned for its interpretations of Beethoven, Brahms, and Schubert.

The back of the viola is made from two pieces of maple, with the sides made of the same wood as the back and the top made from two pieces of spruce. The elegantly carved scroll is made of plain maple. The instrument is varnished in an orange brown color.

IX.

NICOLÒ AMATI

(1642)

WILLEKE

ONCE OWNED BY Institute of Musical Arts faculty member Willem Willeke, a famous Hungarian cellist who played chamber music with Brahms in Vienna, this instrument was donated to Juilliard in 1954 by the Eda K. Loeb Fund. It was used for a time by Claus Adam, the cellist of the Juilliard String Quartet from 1955-1974.

X.

ANTONIO STRADIVARI
(1719)

DUKE OF MARLBOROUGH

THIS INSTRUMENT WAS donated to Juilliard by Daniel and Eleanore Saidenberg in 1999. Mr. and Mrs. Saidenberg were art collectors who owned the Saidenberg Gallery and served as Picasso's chief American representatives from 1955-1973. Mr. Saidenberg, a Juilliard alumnus, was also a cellist and conductor.

The following excerpt from the diary of Arthur F. Hill, dated March 3, 1892, provides some of the instrument's early provenance and lends credence to the widely accepted theory that the belly of the instrument was at one point replaced with one made by a member of the Gagliano family: "George Hart called and mentioned that the Strad. cello dated 1719 which we have now obtained from the Camposelice collection was the one they bought off Capt. Bayley of Exeter. He also stated that the belly was originally of a yellow color, and they thought that this part was made by one of the Gagliano's [sic]. Hart also thought his uncle [William] Valentine had varnished it to match the rest."[1]

Arthur Hill's earliest notes on the instrument indicate that it was sold on the Hills' behalf in 1892 by their German colleague Fridolin Hamma to another German dealer named Edler. Edler then sold the cello to Hugo Becker (1863-1941), Robert Hausmann's successor as head of the Berlin Hochschule für Musik. Becker owned the instrument until around 1923, when it passed to cellist Lorenz Lehr.

Despite the fact that neither the belly nor the scroll of the instrument, which was most likely made by Stradivari during a different period, appears to be original, the instrument is one of the most valuable in Juilliard's collection.

[1] Arthur F. Hill, *Diaries, 1890 – 1939* (London: Unpublished), cited in written note to the author from Robert Bein.

XI.

GAND & BERNARDEL FRÈRES

(1877)

T*HIS INSTRUMENT WAS* one of several double basses made by Gand & Bernardel for the orchestra of Paris's Opéra-Comique. Notable for its fine craftsmanship and handsome lion's head scroll, it was purchased by Juilliard in 1949 from Wurlitzer.

OTHER INSTRUMENTS OF
SPECIAL HISTORICAL INTEREST

XII.

CARLO BERGONZI

(1723)

THIS VIOLIN WAS donated to Juilliard by Mrs. Cordelia Lee Beattie. An announcement of the donation in the *Juilliard News Bulletin* of February, 1964 reads, "Mrs. Beattie, who at one time was quite a renowned violinist in Europe, acquired the violin many years ago from Jacques Thibaud. Mr. Thibaud began his career in a Paris café, but during his first year he was taken into the Colonne orchestra. He soon became a well-known performer in Europe and the United States. He eventually acquired a Stradivarius, but his career was built with this Bergonzi."

XIII.

CARLO ANTONIO TESTORE

(1739)

JUILLIARD PURCHASED THIS violin in 1952 from faculty member Hans Letz. A William E. Hill certificate from 1939 indicates the owner at that time as A. Warshasky, Esq., of Addison Gardens, and describes the instrument as follows: "The back, in two pieces, is marked by a faint small curl; that of the sides is more pronounced, the head being plain. The table, of pine, of open grain. The varnish of a golden-brown colour. This violin is a characteristic example of the maker's work and is in a good state of preservation."

XIV.

GIOVANNI BATTISTA GUADAGNINI

(1754)

EX YSAŸE

THIS VIOLIN WAS was donated to Juilliard by violinist Ralph Hollander in 2006. Mr. Hollander is the inventor of the Dampit, a specially designed humidifier for stringed instruments.

The instrument is named after the famous Belgian violinist Eugène Ysaÿe (1858-1931). According to an article from a 1902 issue of *Music* magazine (reprinted in *The Etude* in September 1909), Ysaÿe first saw the violin in the window of a pawnbroker's shop in Hamburg. Although he was too "young and poor" to afford it, he asked the pawnbroker to set it aside for him. Providentially, an old friend from Belgium arrived in town that very day, and told Ysaÿe that he would have loaned him the money to purchase the violin if only he'd had enough with him. His desire for the instrument overriding his tact, Ysaÿe then asked his friend, a diamond dealer, if he would "just leave a few diamonds as security and get me the Guadagnini." Overcoming his initial shock, the friend agreed. "In this way," Ysaÿe told the interviewer, "I was married to my first love among fiddles – my beautiful Guadagnini."[1]

In 1895, Ysaÿe acquired his famous 1740 Guarneri del Gesù violin and sold the Guadagnini to Paul Nothomb. A note from Ysaÿe concerning the sale, one of several documents Mr. Hollander obtained when he purchased the violin, is reproduced in the Appendix. The violin later found its way to New York, where it was owned by Mrs. Edwin Harris and passed to her children, Edwin Harris, Jr. and Glory Harris. In 1951, the Harris siblings entered into a legal agreement to rent the violin to Mr. Hollander for the sum of $1.00 a year. This arrangement continued for the next 23 years, until Mr. Hollander purchased the violin from Glory Harris Banks in 1974.

---

[1] The brief article is reproduced in Ernest N. Doring, *The Guadagnini Family of Violin Makers* (Chicago: W. Lewis, 1949), 128-29.

XV.

GIOVANNI BATTISTA GUADAGNINI

(1755)

THIS INSTRUMENT WAS purchased by Juilliard from Emil Herrmann in 1950. Mr. Herrmann's certificate refers to the violin as the "ex Weder" and describes its physical characteristics as follows: "The back is of two pieces of handsome maple of wide even curl, the sides to match, the scroll of smaller figure and somewhat different in character than usual. The varnish is of a dark plum red color and plentiful. A good and characteristic example of the Master's Milano period and in a fine state of preservation."

XVI.
GIOVANNI BATTISTA GUADAGNINI
(1765)

DONATED TO JUILLIARD in 2002 by faculty member Margaret Pardee, this instrument was previously owned by Robert Mann, founder and first violinist (until 1997) of the Juilliard String Quartet. A 1902 certificate of authenticity from Caressa & Français indicates a Mr. Gèrard of Geneva as the violin's owner at that time.

Measuring 13 15/16 inches in length, the instrument has a back formed of two pieces of close-grained maple with irregular figure ascending slightly from the joint and a top of medium-grain spruce; the ribs are of similar material to the back.

XVII.

GIOVANNI BATTISTA GUADAGNINI

(1775)

THIS VIOLIN WAS donated to Juilliard in 1950 by Sam Bloomfield. President of the Swallow Airplane Company, Inc. in Wichita, Kansas, Mr. Bloomfield was also a violinist who served as Chairman of the Finance Committee of the Wichita Symphony and helped develop the music department at the University of Kansas. A press release announcing the gift stated that the instrument had been assigned to the Juilliard String Quartet for use in its concert engagements and recordings.

A 1930 certificate of authenticity from Lyon & Healy indicates the instrument's previous owner as Mr. T. Duncan Stewart of Kansas City, Missouri.

Varnished in a reddish brown color, the violin has a back formed by two pieces of maple, with sides to match, and a top made from fine-grained spruce. The scroll is made of plain walnut.

XVIII.

GIOVANNI BATTISTA GUADAGNINI

(1780)

EX KOCHANSKI

T*HIS VIOLIN WAS* purchased by Juilliard in 1935 from the estate of faculty member Paul Kochanski. It was used by alumnus Earl Carlyss, a Juilliard faculty member and former member of the Juilliard String Quartet, when he was a student.

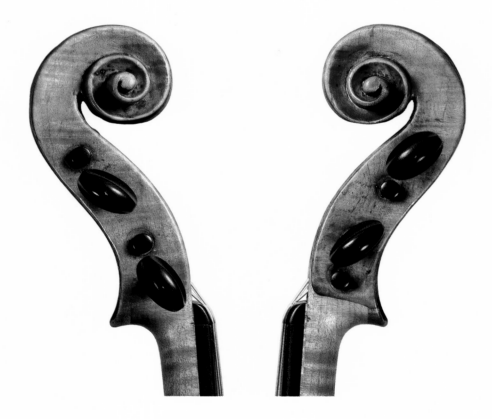

XIX.

JULIO CESARE GIGLI

(1762)

THIS VIOLA WAS purchased by Juilliard in 1938 from Emil Herrmann. Mr. Herrmann's certificate offers the following description of the instrument: "The back is of two pieces of curly maple of rather indistinct figure, the sides to match, and the scroll of plain wood. The table is of spruce of rather wide grain. The varnish is of a golden brown color."

XX.

CARLO MANTEGAZZA

(fl. ca. 1750-90)

THIS VIOLA WAS donated to Juilliard in 1953 by Regina Wynne. Since this instrument bears no label, its date cannot be precisely determined. It has a two-piece back and medium-grain spruce top, with a light golden varnish. The two wooden nails in the back are a distinctive feature.

XXI.

GAETANO SGARABOTTO

(1907)

THE BACK OF this viola is cut on the quarter from two pieces of maple, while the top is made from two pieces of spruce. Its scroll is cut on the slab. The instrument also exhibits unusual chisel scoring on its C-bout and upper rib. Its varnish is a brownish orange color and its length is 16 5/8 inches.

XXII.

LORENZO AND TOMASO CARCASSI

(fl. ca. 1750-80)

T HE VIOLA D'AMORE was a type of viola popular during the late 17th and 18th centuries. The soundholes on this model are in the "flaming sword" shape typical for this category of instrument.

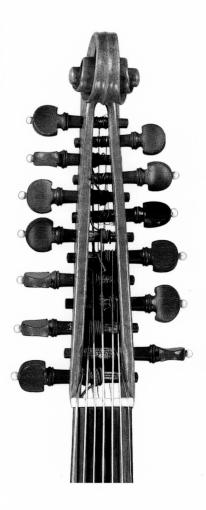

XXIII.

PAOLO ANTONIO TESTORE

(1750)

THE DATE AND method of acquisition for this instrument are unknown, but it was in Juilliard's possession by December, 1961. It was loaned to cellist Bion Tsang when he was a student in Juilliard's Pre-College Division.

The back is one piece of poplar, and the wood is slab-cut.

XIV.

JOSÉ CONTRERAS

MADRID (1756)

THIS CELLO WAS purchased by Juilliard in 1938 from Emil Herrmann. Mr. Herrmann's certificate includes the following observations about the instrument: "The back is in two pieces of maple of pretty, small, even curl, the sides to match. The top of pine of medium grain. The varnish of an ordinary orange color and all original. A very fine and characteristic specimen of this great Spanish master's work, in a high state of preservation."

XXV.

Carlo Tononi

(1700)

DESIGNATED AS THE Gabriele Wunderlich Memorial Cello, this instrument was purchased by Juilliard from Jacques Français in 1993 with funds from the estate of Gabriele Wunderlich. It was previously owned by cellist Barbara Levy.

The cello has several notable features: the wood is slab-cut, the top is made from three pieces of spruce, and the back is from one piece of poplar. The varnish is a dark reddish brown.

IMPORTANT BOWS
IN THE COLLECTION

FRANÇOIS XAVIER TOURTE

(ca. 1795)

THIS BOW WAS donated to Juilliard by Ralph Hollander.

Noting its round stick in beautiful dark reddish-brown pernambuco wood, ebony frog mounted with a silver ferrule, and whitish-blue mother-of-pearl slide and heel, a certificate of authenticity from Bernard Millant, Paris (dated February 13, 1984) praises this violin bow as "a beautiful specimen of the 'Stradivarius of bows.'"

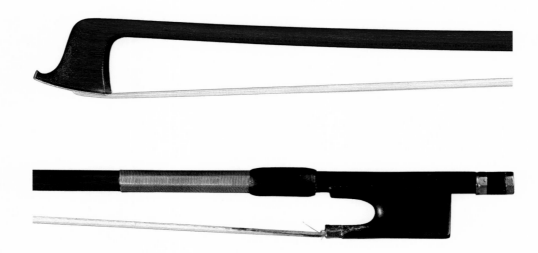

VICTOR FÉTIQUE

(ca. 1925)

THIS VIOLIN BOW was donated to Juilliard by Annette Mark. It has a round stick and features a gold mounted ivory frog with Parisian eyes. The button is inlaid with eight ivory facets.

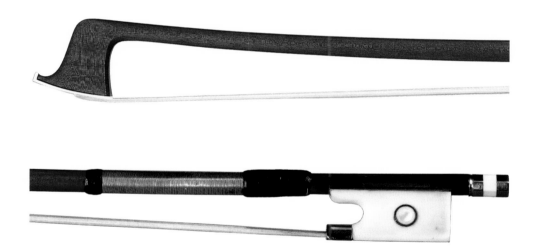

Nicolas Leonard Tourte

(ca. 1785-90)

THIS RARE TRANSITIONAL swanhead violin bow was donated to Juilliard by Ralph Hollander. It has a round stick made of dark reddish-brown pernambuco wood and an ivory frog. It remains in its original state without an ivory headplate, and the head mortice is unaltered.

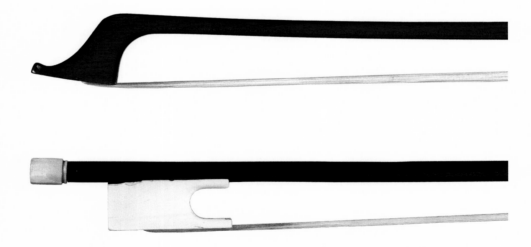

Annotated List of
Select Instruments and Bows

ANNOTATED LIST OF
SELECT INSTRUMENTS AND BOWS

T*HIS LIST REPRESENTS* the core of Juilliard's stringed instrument collection and includes approximately 100 instruments and 30 bows. Juilliard is also the grateful owner of several dozen additional instruments and bows which, while less valuable monetarily than those listed below, are of great benefit to its students.

The author sincerely regrets any errors or omissions that may have occurred in the preparation of this list.

Amati, Nicolò	Cello	1642	*Donated by the Eda K. Loeb Fund*
Amati, Girolamo	Violin	1690	*Donated anonymously*
American unknown	Viola	1960	*Donated by Joseph DiFiore*
Bassot, Joseph	Violin		
Berger, Karl August	Violin	1947	*Donated by Dorothy DeLay*
Bergonzi, Carlo	Violin	1723	*Donated by Cordelia Lee Beattie*
Bergonzi, Carlo	Violin	1733	*Donated by Albert Spalding*
Bergonzi, Carlo (composite)	Violin		*Donated by Paul Whitten*
Bisiach, Carlo	Violin	1924	*Gift from the Estate of Darius Rastomji*
Boianciuc, Roman	Bass	2000	*Purchased with donated funds*
Boianciuc, Roman	Bass	2002	*Purchased with donated funds*
Boianciuc, Roman	Bass	2002	*Purchased with donated funds*
Carcassi, Lorenzo and Tomaso	Viola d'amore	1783	
Ceruti, Giovanni Battista	Violin (1/2 size)	1810	*Donated by Margaret Pardee*
Chanot, George	Violin		
Contreras, José	Cello	1765	*Purchased with donated funds*
Cuniot-Hury	Violin Bow		
Deconet, Michele	Violin	1730	*Donated by Lawrence Morris*
Dutch	Violin (7/8 size)	1800	*Donated by Margaret Pardee*
English, Chris	Quartet of Transitional Bows	1980	
Erdesz, Otto	Viola		

Fagnola, Hannibal	Violin		
Farotto, Celeste	Viola	1925	
Fétique, Victor	Cello Bow	1920	*Donated by Robert Stein, M.D.*
Fétique, Victor	Violin Bow	ca. 1925	*Donated by Annette C. Mark*
Forster, Simon	Cello		*Donated by Benjamin Hertzberg*
French	Viola	1800s	
Friedel, Heinrich August	Cello	1937	
Gagliano, Alessandro	Violin	1700	*Donated by Maurice Levine*
Gagliano, Gennaro	Violin	1765	*Donated by Annette C. Mark*
Gagliano, Giuseppe and Antonio	Violin	1806	
Gagliano, Nicolò	Violin	1737	*Purchased with donated funds*
Gand & Bernardel	Bass	1877	*Purchased with donated funds*
Gand	Violin	1840	
Gemünder	Violin	1897	*Donated by Walter Hespee*
Gemünder	Cello	1897	
Gemünder	Bass		
German	Viola	1800s	*Donated by Garett J. Albert*
Gigli, Julio Cesare	Viola	1762	*Purchased with donated funds*
Gofriller, Francesco	Violin	1734	
Gonzalez, Fernando Solar	Viola	1973	*Donated by maker*
Grancino, Michelangelo	Cello	1800	*Donated by Nancy Isear*
Grancino, Giovanni	Viola	1699	*Purchased with donated funds*
Guadagnini, Giovanni Battista I	Violin	1715	
Guadagnini, Giovanni Battista II	Violin	1754	*Donated by Ralph Hollander*
Guadagnini, Giovanni Battista II	Violin	1755	*Purchased with donated funds*
Guadagnini, Giovanni Battista II	Violin	1765	*Donated by Margaret Pardee*
Guadagnini, Giovanni Battista II	Violin	1775	*Donated by Sam Bloomfield*
Guadagnini, Giovanni Battista II	Violin	1780	*Purchased with donated funds from the Estate of Paul Kochanski*
Guarneri del Gesù, Giuseppe	Violin	1729	*Donated by Howard Phipps, Jr.*
Guarneri del Gesù, Giuseppe	Violin	1731	*Donated anonymously*
Guarneri del Gesù, Giuseppe	Violin	1731-34	*Intended legacy of Louise Behrend*
Guarneri de Gesù, Giuseppe	Violin	1740-43	*Donated anonymously*
Guarneri, Pietro of Venice	Violin	1721	*Donated by Mrs. Samuel Grimson*
Gutter, Fritz	Violin Bow		

Gutter, George Walter	Viola	1920	
Gutter, George Walter	Viola	1925	
Heaps, Alfred Walter	Cello	1897	
Hill, William E. & Sons	Violin Bow		*Donated by Avery Fisher*
Hummel, Mathias	Bass	1789	
Jacquot	Bass		*Donated by Walter Damrosch*
Jacquot	Bass		
Kessler, Ernst	Violin	1900	
Klotz, Joseph	Violin	1807	*Donated by Marvin Epstein*
Kolstein	Viola Bow		*Donated by Margaret Pardee*
Kolstein	Viola Bow		*Donated by Margaret Pardee*
Kolstein	Violin Bow		*Donated by Margaret Pardee*
Kreuzinger, Friedrich	Viola da Gamba	1972	
Lamy, Alfred Joseph	Violin Bow		*Donated by Francis Wolf*
Lamy, Alfred Joseph	Violin Bow		*Donated by Francis Wolf*
Mantegazza, Carlo	Viola		*Donated by Regina Wynne*
Mariani, Antonio	Viola	1629	*Donated by William Kruskal*
Marvin, Stephen	Quartet of Baroque bows		*Purchased with donated funds*
Marvin, Stephen	Quartet of Transitional Bows		*Purchased with donated funds*
Millant, Bernard	Viola Bow	1950	*Donated by Samuel Rhodes*
Mougenot	Cello		
Mougenot	Cello		
Neapolitan	Violin	1845	*Donated by Margaret Pardee*
Nürnberger, Franz Albert	Violin Bow		*Donated by Walter Seidl*
Nürnberger, Franz Albert	Violin Bow		*Donated by Margaret Pardee*
Oppelt, Richard	Violin	1989	
Ouchard	Viola Bow		*Donated by Margaret Pardee*
Panarmo, George Louis	Violin	1825	*Purchased with donated funds*
Peccatte	Violin Bow		*Gift from the Estate of Helen Marshall Woodward*
Pfretzschner	Bass		*Donated by John E. Grossman*
Pfretzschner	Bass	1920	*Donated by John E. Grossman*
Pfretzschner	Cello Bow		*Donated by Blanche Hilf*
Piccagliani, Armando	Violin	1926	*Donated by Albert Tannenbaum*
Pierray, Claude	Cello	1714	*Donated by Robert Stein, M.D.*

Pressenda, Gian Francesco	Violin		*Donated by Margaret Pardee*
Pressenda, Gian Francesco	Violin	1844	*Purchased with donated funds*
Pressenda, Gian Francesco	Violin		
Rocca, Giuseppe Antonio	Viola	1854	*Gift from the estate of Audrey Fischer*
Rottenburgh, Jan H. Joseph	Violin	1751	*Unknown donor*
Salchow, William	Violin Bow	1962	*Gift from the Estate of Helen Marshall Woodward*
Sartory, Eugène	Violin Bow	1900	*Gift from the Estate of Mary H. Brown*
Scarampella label	Violin	1900	
Sgarabotto, Gaetano	Viola	1907	*Purchased with donated funds*
So, Vanna	Viola	1997	*Donated by Margaret Pardee*
Sofritti, Ettore	Violin	1900	*Donated by Emery Pillitzest*
Stradivari, Antonio	Violin	1692	*Donated by Avery Fisher*
Stradivari, Antonio	Cello	1719	*Donated by Daniel and Eleanore Saidenberg*
Stradivari, Antonio	Violin	1728	*Donated by Leopold Godowsky, Jr.*
Strnad, Kaspar	Cello		*Donated by Blanche Hilf*
Tarr, William	Cello	1875	
Testore, Carlo Antonio	Violin		*Donated by the Estate of Ruth Evans Morris*
Testore, Carlo Antonio	Violin	1739	*Purchased with donated funds*
Testore, Paolo Antonio	Cello	1756	
Thier, Mathias	Cello		*Donated by Ralph Hollander*
Tononi, Carlos	Cello	1700	*Purchased with funds from the Estate of Gabriele Wunderlich*
Tourte, Louis	Violin Bow	Mid-18th century	*Donated by Ralph Hollander*
Tourte, François Xavier	Violin Bow	Late 18th century	*Donated by Ralph Hollander*
Tubbs	Violin Bow		*Gift from the Estate of Audrey Fischer*
Valenzano, Giovanni Maria	Violin	1825	*Donated by Dr. Leopold Reiner*
Varotti, Giovanni	Violin	1798	
Voirin	Cello Bow		*Donated by Benjamin Hertzberg*
Voirin	Violin Bow		*Gift from the Estate of Audrey Fischer*
Voirin	Violin Bow		*Gift from the Estate of Audrey Fischer*
Vuillaume, Jean-Baptiste	Violin	1864	*Gift from the Estate of Helen Marshall Woodward*
Vuillaume, Jean-Baptiste	Violin	1840	*Donated by Ellen Taafe Zwilich*
Yamimoto, Tohru	Violin	1981	*Donated by Dorothy DeLay*

APPENDIX:
LETTERS AND CERTIFICATES
OF AUTHENTICITY

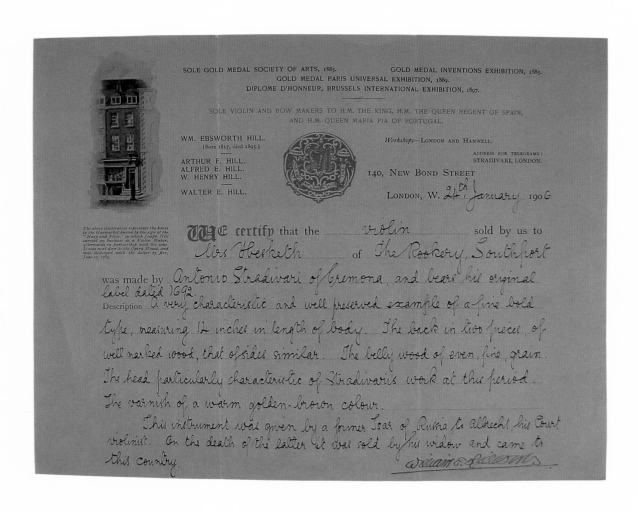

Stradivari (1692), *Avery Fisher:*
certificate from William E. Hill & Sons, dated January 24, 1906

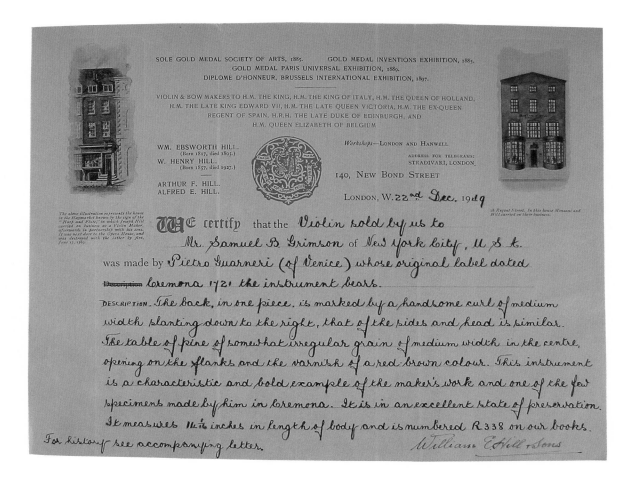

Pietro Guarneri (1721), *Grimson Guarneri:*
certificate from William E. Hill & Sons, dated December 22, 1919

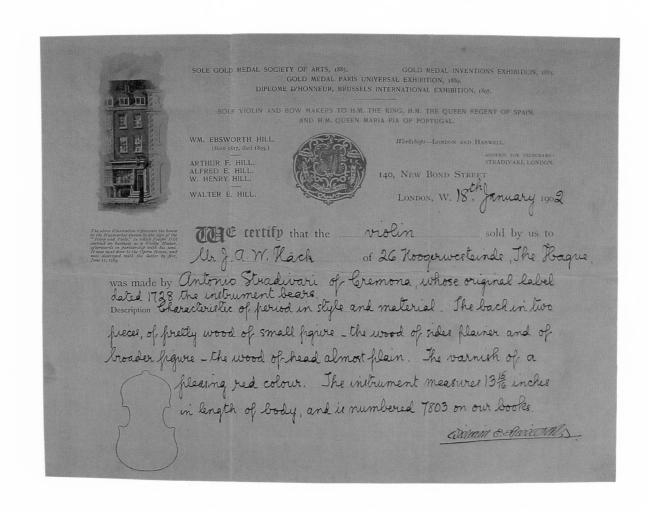

Stradivari (1728), *Artôt:*
certificate from William E. Hill & Sons, dated January 18, 1902

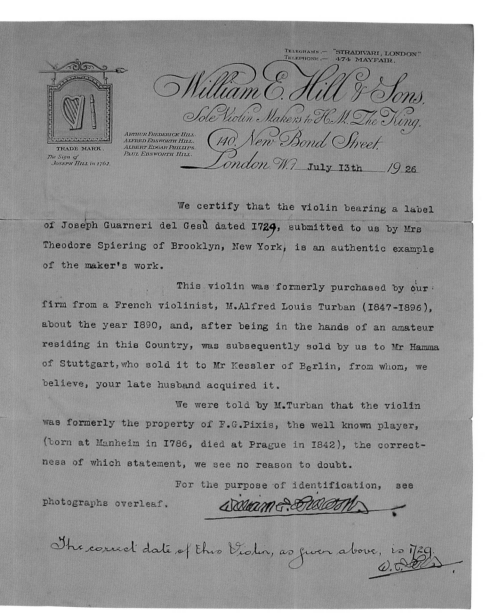

Guarneri del Gesù (1729), *Pixis:*
certificate from William E. Hill & Sons, dated July 13, 1926

Guarneri del Gesù (1731), *Mayseder Guarnerius:*
letter from Arthur F. Hill to Maude Powell, dated December 11, 1903

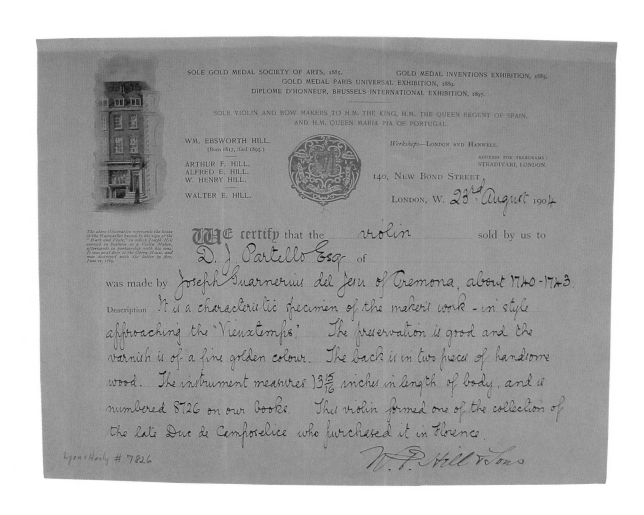

Guarneri del Gesù (1740-43), *Duc de Camposelice:*
certificate from William E. Hill & Sons, dated August 23, 1904

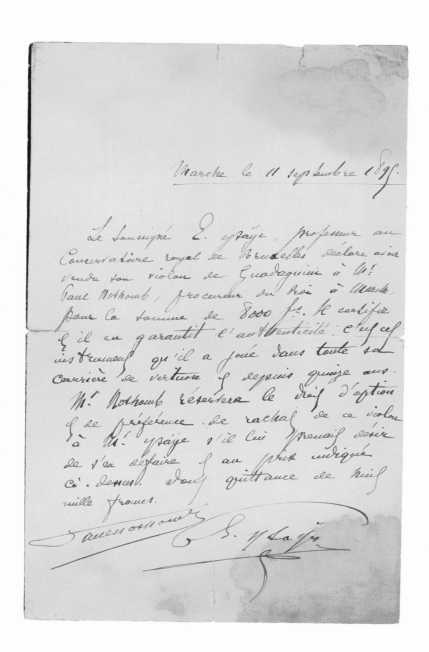

Giovanni Battista Guadagnini (1754),
note by Eugène Ysaÿe regarding instrument

BIBLIOGRAPHY

Bachmann, Alberto. *An Encyclopedia of the Violin.* Original introduction by Eugene Ysaÿe. Translated by Frederick H. Martens. London: D. Appleton Century Company, 1937; Reprint, New York: Da Capo Press, 1966.

Balfoort, Dirk J. *Antonio Stradivarius.* Translated by W.A.G. Doyle-Davidson. Stockholm: The Continental Book Co., n.d.

Bein & Fushi, Inc., eds. *The Miracle Makers.* Chicago: Bein and Fushi, 1998.

Boyden, David. *The History of the Violin from Its Origins to 1761 and Its Relationship to the Violin and Violin Music.* New York: Oxford University Press, 1990.

Burgess, David, et al. "Forum – Oberlin College Program." *Journal of the Violin Society of America* 18, no. 3 (2003): 25-47.

Chiesa, Carlo. *The Stradivari Legacy.* London: Peter Biddulph, 1998.

Doring, Ernest N. *The Guadagnini Family of Violin Makers.* Chicago: W. Lewis, 1949.

Henley, William and Cyril Woodcock. *Universal Dictionary of Violin and Bow Makers,* 2d ed. Brighton, Eng.: Amati Pub., 1965-73.

Hill, W. Henry, Arthur F., and Alfred E. *The Violin Makers of the Guarneri Family.* London: W. E. Hill & Sons, 1931; Reprint, New York: Dover Publications, Inc., 1991.

_____. *Antonio Stradivari: His Life and Work.* London: W. E. Hill & Sons, 1902; Reprint, New York: Dover Publications, Inc., 1963.

Instrument Records, The Juilliard School Archives, Juilliard School Library, New York, N.Y.

Jalovec, Karel. *Beautiful Italian Violins.* Translated by J.B. Kozak. London: P. Hamlyn, 1963.

_____. *Encyclopedia of Violin Makers.* Translated by J.B. Kozak. Edited by Patrick Hanks. 2 vols. London: P. Hamlyn, 1965.

_____. *German and Austrian Violinmakers.* Translated by George Theiner. Edited by Patrick Hanks. London: P. Hamlyn, 1967.

_____. *Italian Violinmakers,* rev. ed. Translated by B. Wiener. London: P. Hamlyn, 1964.

_____. *The Violin Makers of Bohemia, including Craftsmen of Moravia and Slovakia.* London: Anglo-Italian Publications, 1959.

Libin, Laurence, et al. "Instruments, Collections of," *New Grove Online,* ed. L. Macy (accessed 28 June 2005) <http//www. Grovemusic.com>

Lyon & Healy. *Catalog of Rare Old Violins, Violas & Violoncellos and Bows of Rare Makers in the Collection of Lyon & Healy*, Chicago, 33rd ed. Chicago: Lyon & Healy, 1922.

Pollens, Stewart. "Messiah Redux." *Journal of The Violin Society of America* 17, no. 3 (2001): 159-179.

Regazzi, Roberto. The Complete Luthier's Library: a Useful International Critical Bibliography for the Maker and Connoisseur of Stringed and Plucked Instruments. Bologna: Florenus Edizioni, 1990.

Sadie, Stanley, ed. *The New Grove Dictionary of Musical Instruments.* 3 vols. London: MacMillan, 1984.

Vannes, René, ed. *Dictionnaire Universel des Luthiers.* Bruxelles: Les amis de la musique, 1951.

NOTES FROM THE PHOTOGRAPHER

THE JUILLIARD SCHOOL'S collection of stringed instruments represented in this book was photographed in the spring of 2004, over two sessions consisting of two days each. The photography took place on site at the School.

My equipment comprised Lowel Tota-Light and Pro-Light lamps, with the former fitted with 500 watt Tungsten bulbs and the latter fitted with 250 watt Tungsten bulbs. The tops and scrolls were photographed using diffusion umbrellas, whereas the backs were photographed with hard light. A multicolored Schneider Apo-Symmar 6.8/360 mm lens mounted in a Copal 3 shutter was used in front of the Sinar P2 4x5 view camera. The images were captured on Tungsten balanced Kodak EPY color reversal film.

As a violinmaker as well as a photographer, I honed my craft of instrument photography partly for selfish reasons – namely, because it affords me the opportunity to be among such fine objects as those represented in this book. My goal is to capture archivally the live essence of each instrument, so that you may enjoy the presence of this fine and generously gifted collection.

– Tucker Densley